HOW TO COUNSEL THE BATTERED WOMEN IN THE CHURCH

Adrianne D. Brady, Revised 2018

Original Copyright© 1998 by Adrianne D. Brady
ISBN: 978-0-9646442-2-3 February 2018
Library of Congress Control Number:

Published by Adrianne Brady Publishing

Original Edits by: Angela Brady
Revision Edits by: Apostle Adrianne Brady, Angela Moore

Revised Edition 2018 Edits by Ronda Buckmon, Angela Moore and Marilyn Brower

Revised Edition Cover Design and Book Format by CreateSpace

The Thompson Chain-Reference Bible

Fifth Improved Edition Commentary:
Matthew Henry Commentary unless otherwise noted.

Printed in the United States of America
How To Counsel the Battered Woman in the Church

Author:202-644-6741
email: adriannebrady@yahoo.com

2nd Revised Edition 2018
2nd Print

Table of Contents

DEDICATION

I dedicate this book to my Mom, Judythe Collins Richardson, my late husband Roy W. Brady, my late son Adrian Roy Brady, and my family. Through my many struggles and challenges, you inspired me to keep pressing to reach the highest mark that I could accomplish. Because of each of you I have completed one of the many phases of my life that I have longed to complete.

IF I CAN HELP SOMEBODY ALONG LIFE'S WAY, THEN I KNOW MY LABOR IS NOT IN VAIN.

Mahalia Jackson

THANK YOU.

INTRODUCTION

It's been twenty-nine years since the Lord delivered me from the abusive relationship. I have been blessed to have re-established my life, renewed my relationship in Christ and am walking in liberty where I am made free. Over the years there have been many challenges in preparing this book to be a guide to those who are still victims and cannot find solace in the local church. The church has yet to address this issue face to face and to make a significant impact in our communities by openly addressing this issue and providing a safe haven for its members. While there has been an increase of domestic violence incidents, some States have taken an active role in leading task forces for prevention and to ensure perpetrators and victims receive the help they need. Laws have been instituted to include mandatory arrest even when the victim doesn't want to press charges. (This can be tricky based on who has the visual marks or appear to be the aggressor, an erroneous arrest can be made leaving the most dangerous person in the public).

As for the church, there have been more incidents of abuse and the need for outreach is prevalent, however it is still not addressed in a manner and a level where people are free to expose what is happening. Churches have allowed for seminars and workshops to bring awareness and this is a huge step. Many are openly speaking about abuse from the pulpit but there is still not enough being done. The major problem of today is that we are not being honest about where we are. Many are still in denial that abuse is learned behavior.

Until we are as comfortable with making it an issue as we do with sins that are clearly addressed, such as sexual sins, alcohol and drug addictions, we are allowing it to be the hidden agenda of satan to divide families through the spirit of control. This needs to be exposed from the pulpit to the pews.

The purpose of this book is to assist those who minister to victims of domestic violence in their local churches and are looking for a resource to guide them. There are many references and publications that have been written on this issue, but not enough that directly share or propose churches viewpoints and plans of action. This type of ministry is not very popular but is in high demand. The evidence of this conclusion is the rise of violence that is now plaguing our communities. Violence begat violence and children who have watched this type of communication and behavior while they were young are now exemplifying what they were taught and even worse. This is a ministry that can no longer be avoided and I pray that my transparency of what I experienced can give insight on how the church can assist in addressing this issue more directly.

It is time now for the body of Christ to get in place and Minister to those men and women who are seeking a word of deliverance to take back our families.

THE BATTERED WOMAN IN THE CHURCH

The woman in the church has suffered for many years, and has been faithful in her belief that she should stay in that relationship in obedience to the word of God concerning her marital status. Many have survived by going to church on a regular basis while hiding her bruises and distress. She depends on her prayers and doing whatever she could to make sure her husband is satisfied which keeps him preoccupied with other things. Many women who I have had the opportunity to speak with said that many times alcohol ignited the violence in their home, and their husbands were not church goers. Some shared that their husband were the head of the home, and the bread winner and whatever he told her to do, it should be. This scenario was due to women not being able to take care of themselves. Women were often told by their church leaders and mothers of the church to stay there and make sure they don't give *"that man a hard time"*.

In the Church, there are women from different backgrounds who are going through some of the same issues and are seeking a word from God. Women who are victims of domestic violence and have a relationship with God are doing everything possible to hold on to their faith and the word of God. Unfortunately, there is very little information that would give her specific instructions to get out of that relationship without her feeling that she has

1

dishonored God, or that she is disobeying God if she leaves her husband.

The U.S. Department of Justice, statistics suggest that domestic violence account for 21% of all violent crime. Knowing this has led me to believe that the percentage is just as great among those who are considered believers in the body of Christ. This is a very difficult survey to take due to the many who are afraid to expose what is happening in their homes.

IDENTIFYING

CHARACTERISTICS

This chapter is not written to imply that you will be able to go into your local church and start pointing out people who are abused based on the examples used. This is guidance and is designed to give you suggestions as to how to observe someone who may be exemplifying these signs. Don't assume. The abuser in the church can be anyone. He is not out front for all to see. The victim is low key and praying that someone reaches out to her. In doing so, the approaching the issue concerning her should be welcoming.

There are four types of scenarios of battered women in the church that I would like to address.

- **The saved woman who is married to a saved abusive spouse,**
- **The saved woman married to an officer or leader in the church who is abusive,**
- **The saved woman married to an unsaved spouse and,**
- **The saved woman dating an abusive person.**

Each of these situations may be different but they are all seeking a response to the same questions. Saved and Abused, Must I Obey? Or How Can I Get Out? Some may say the woman who is dating an abusive person can get out faster since they are not married, but sometimes these are

3

the toughest relationships to break, each woman in one of these four scenarios operates out of fear.

Saved with a saved abusive spouse

This is especially difficult if the abuser is the Pastor. In some instances, if she is the Pastor's wife, she has been told that revealing the abuse will make her responsible for dividing and destroying the church. If the spouse is not clergy, then she feels she has an obligation to stay according to the word of God. Many are taught that God hates divorce and this is why she is more compelled to stay than to leave. Over the years there have been stories told of how some marriages stayed together, however, every situation is different. She has been told that this is family business and that her position is to back him up and keep their private affairs out of the church. This makes it difficult for her to come forward and stand in the backlash that she will receive. She feels obligated to stay. She is usually not very verbal and is often defined as being sweet, gentile and quiet.

Saved and Married to Clergy, Officer in the Church

This woman has an expectancy that God will change things for her. She is constantly praying that this will not continue and that God answers her prayers. The challenge for her is that there are others watching and she is told that her role is to be an example to the women of the church. She may be married to a minister, deacon, pastor, clergy official or member of the local church but her outlook is towards what the word of God says for her marriage. This abuse can be physical, mental, or verbal, but it is still labeled abuse.   Women who are married to clergy tend to suffer the most because they have the most to lose. She also knows that many women are looking up to her and she feels a spiritual obligation to portray a positive image. At least that is what they are told.   Some have told their stories, and some have even shot and killed their abuser (yes, a Pastor).   Whatever it takes, I believe she is now willing to take a stand for peace sake.

(Special Testimony) My ex-husband was serving as an Elder in our local church when I met him. The abuse started immediately after marriage. It was very difficult for me to share, even with the Pastor, when I knew that my husband had a reputation of being a God-fearing man. It's not just his shame but yours as well. When you are married to clergy there is a standard that a woman believes that God holds her too. There is not only an obligation to her family but to the church of God. It is the first and foremost reverential fear that she is placed with in sharing the abuse with anyone. Her allegiance is to the position as well as fear of violating principles of God's law where the family is concerned. (Even, if what she believes isn't true. It is very difficult to reveal what is happening when it can be the very thing that destroys the local assembly.

Saved with an unsaved abusive spouse

This scenario can be very challenging.   There is the obligation of following the guidance of an unsaved man and obeying the word of God. Obeying the abuser appears to be the rational decision to make since she is being forced by physical violence and/or threats thereof. Although she is taught that she should obey God rather than man; this can be used to keep the attention of her situation away from those with whom she fellowships. The woman who is married to an unsaved man has a hard time differentiating between the submission to her husband and God. She is looking for clarity from the word of God when she comes to church.

(Special Testimony) I spoke to a woman who told me that her husband forbade her to go to church at times. He often accused her of being unfaithful and spending too much time at the church. She shared that he was a drinker and would often fight her before and sometimes after church, however; it all stopped when he got too old to hit her anymore without hurting himself. She suffered a long time and is still married to him.

(Special Testimony) A woman shared with me how her husband would fight her and she was Pastoring a church. One time he went to hit her and he had a heart attack. She came to me to ask if she could get a divorce. He never hit her again.

Many women who are saved and are married to an unsaved come to church specifically to find refuge. Unfortunately, they very seldom receive what God's intentions are but rather opinions from those who have been in the same relationship and stayed there. These women have come out either because the abuser is sick or too old to fight. The scripture that God revealed to me in this situation is Matthew 10:28, do not be afraid of those who kill the body but cannot kill the soul. Most of the women who stayed in this type of marriage stayed for fear.

Dating an Unsaved Person

Most of the time, abuse is overlooked and forgiven at this stage. If a woman told the truth, there are incidents and issues that show up before the couple decides to marry. However, if it is not physical (and sometimes it is) it is minimized by stress, substance abuse or an emotion that justifies his actions. This is not to say that a woman is in denial or does not see it, it is because this behavior generally doesn't appear until her heart is in the relationship and she can be easily persuaded by his justifications. This person is probably dating the man that she believes is going to be her husband. As a single woman, she too has to make the decision to portray godliness in all that she does. When dating she should be aware that getting into compromising situations can give a perpetrator room for control. This is a time when the signs of domestic violence can go unnoticed. Women who are waiting on God to bless her with a husband will interpret his overprotective, jealous behavior as love. Isolation from family and friends can make her feel as though she is special to him and wants to spend all of his time with her. This is a dangerous area because as the scripture says, "in a multitude of counsellors there is safety" Proverbs 15:22. This is an opportunity for him to control her every being and keep others from seeing his insecurities.

The single woman must stay focused. She may have been out of a relationship for a while and has not completely healed from past hurts. This makes her vulnerable for those men who are not secure to prey on her insecurities. Women become mesmerized by the idea of being wanted, needed, and shown special attention to especially if this is a new experience. Sometimes a woman will tolerate a certain behavior because she may have children with the man. If there is a child involved, the obligation she has is to the child and not to him, however she doesn't see it especially if she grew up without her father.

In each of the four scenarios outlined above spiritual abuse is highly evidenced, although it is not always acknowledged or addressed. This is not to say that other forms of abuse are not present. Spiritual abuse is easily observed in the church. It's usually is cloaked under obedience. We must know how to approach her without running her away. More than likely she has done a good job in keeping the attention away from her family, but she longs for a break-through. The perpetrator and the victim will try to hide it as much as possible.

Pastors and Bishops are finding they can no longer overlook the cries of the women in the local church. Many women are coming to the forefront and are tired of suffering in silence. The church has to take a stand and begin to preach from the pulpit a no tolerance for perpetrators of domestic violence in their churches. Women are boldly demanding their place in the Kingdom of God, women are being ordained and consecrated for a time such as this. It is becoming harder to ignore the issue of domestic violence however some women would rather ignore it as well and hope for the best. It's time for clergy to speak up and help these families who are broken.

Men as the Victim

This is not to say that all men abuse or that men are not victims as well because they are. This has been an area that has been swept under the rug for many reasons. Most of the time it's because if a man allows a woman to abuse him then he is considered weak or not a real man. In my experience, men are just as much a victim as women but incident are not counted as with women.

There are no shelters or seminars specifically outlined to help men who are being controlled, physically, and mentally abused by women. He needs to get out of that relationship because he can be the next victim. In ministering in this area there has been men who have come with this issue and want information on how to get this person to change. Their mindset was not wanting to physically fight their wives, although they were being hit. They come looking for a way to stay with her and not feel that they are prevented from being the man that God has called them to be. Many will read this and say that this is a weak man who seeks help from a woman.

Forms of Abuse

Domestic violence is defined as any assault, battery, sexual assault, or any criminal offense resulting in personal injury or death of one family or household member by another, who is or was residing in the same single dwelling unit. "Family or household member" means spouse, former spouse, persons related by blood or by marriage, persons who are presently residing together, as if a family, or who have resided together in the past, as if a family, and persons who have a child in common regardless of whether they have been married or have resided together at any time.

Whenever a woman is placed in physical danger or controlled by the threat or use of physical force, she has been abused. The risk for abuse is greatest when a woman is separated from supportive networks (family, friends, church, work.)

Abuse comes in many forms. If we are to be effective in this ministry we must be able to differentiate the many forms of abuse. Some would say name calling, forbidding her to go to church, choosing her clothes, and taking her money is not abuse. Most of the time if it isn't physical we don't call it abuse.

Physical Abuse – is usually recurrent and escalates. It may include the following. Pushing, shoving, slapping, punching, kicking, or choking. Holding down, tying down, leaving in a dangerous place or refusal to help when sick or injured. Marks, cuts or bruises may be observed. Dark shades are sometimes used to cover black eyes. There may be an unusual increase of clothing.

If the abuse is physical, she dresses to hide it. She can be very despondent and openly depressed. She can also appear to be controlling, defensive and very short with her conversations. However, she tries very hard to keep her head up in effort to hide the abuse.

(Special Testimony) Physical Abuse was the worst in my relationship, this happened every day. The first hit was when I was punched in the eye because someone called the house and had the wrong number. The abuse was evident even when we didn't have a place to live. I was pinched in my hands where people couldn't see what was going on while in meetings. We were staying in a shelter and I was kicked in my private area and had to go the hospital because of passing a blood clot. The physical abuse was always at a peak and never minimal. Incidents lasted all night and all day.

Verbal Abuse – Evidence of a woman being verbally abused would not be easily recognizable. However, some evidence would be cringing when someone yells, or being easily intimidated, despondent and shying away from confrontation. Verbal abuse dictates how her day goes.

(Special Testimony) The verbal abuse was so bad that you start to believe what is being said to you. There were times when I was told very derogatory

things about myself that I felt I was just what was said. (Stories were put together as to tell me how a situation turned out and I just followed the story line, the unfortunate part was that the other person (who I was accused of) wasn't present. This is the step where women are made to feel stupid, dumb, and have no purpose but to be under a man's feet.

Emotional Abuse - This form of abuse can cause instability of one's mind. The victim is often told things that could, should, or might happen. Love is withheld. Mind games, and stress is evident. Extreme jealousy and possessiveness, intimidation and name calling, breaking promises, lying and destroying trust.

(Special Testimony) Emotional abuse made me jump at the sight of people with who I had been accused of being intimate. This was so bad that it was in my sleep, I would dream that he was fighting me and I would wake up and he was hitting me. You become paranoid thinking that people outside of him are after you. I was told that I couldn't speak to anyone at work, well when I came home it was almost as though he was right there with me. He would ask me if anyone had spoken to me that day, then he would drill me as to why it was impossible for people not to. This would start an argument and fight about whether I spoke to someone at work or not. So, at work I was an emotional wreck by avoiding people I knew so they wouldn't say hello.

(Special Testimony) A woman shared with me that her husband/boyfriend would come home from work and run straight to the back door trying to see if he could catch someone leaving.

Sexual Abuse– This form of abuse involves being made to carry out acts that are uncomfortable. Rape (this can be from a husband) is what these acts really are but very rarely identified as. Hurting her physically during sex or assaulting her genitals are used as a form of punishment. This type of behavior is hardly ever mentioned in reports of abuse especially if it is between a husband and a wife. She is made to have sex in different ways, with objects at inopportune times or places. Sometimes made to have sex with other people.

(Special Testimony) The sexual abuse for me was after the fight, he thought that hitting me was not enough punishment. He often wanted to have sex through acts that I was not willing to do and when I resisted he forced me against my will. It didn't matter that the acts were painful. I could never like the sex, if I did, I was told that my reaction is because I have had partners other than men.

Spiritual Abuse – This form of abuse is very seldom addressed. Scriptures are used and are taken out of context to justify many of the actions associated with this form of abuse. The victim is not allowed to freely serve God. She cannot go to church unless he says so. He tries to stop her from praying as she knows and also imposes his form of prayer. He tells her that if she tells anyone about the abuse that she will be responsible for destroying the church.

(Special Testimony) I could no longer go to the church where we first met. He was the head of the house, the man and if I was to speak it could only be to talk about the women in the bible. I was told that my job was to support him. I had to leave the room if a man came to visit him. When the Pastor came over, I wasn't allowed to come out of the room to greet him. That was his job. He selected the church for us to attend.

Spiritual abuse is also found in the church. Leaders who insist individuals in their congregation do things his way instead of Gods way because he is "the pastor" is a form of spiritual abuse. Some use intimidation and scare tactics to get members to continue their membership. There are controlling spirits in the church. If the pastor runs his house with a controlling spirit he will run the church the same way. He is identified as being a very strong leader when he is operating with a controlling spirit. Also, people who have been abused have a greater tendency to become abusive. This type of abusive leader will not only hurt family but hurt his members. Abused individuals come from all walks of life, all races, educational and religious backgrounds. A battered woman can be a cleaning woman or the president of a large corporation, an evangelist, Sunday school teacher or pastor of a church.

Outreach From the Pulpit

People come to church for spiritual guidance and direction to live a successful life. They come seeking answers to their questions to endure struggles and to find peace from their storms. Whatever their situation may be, the church should always be ready to help.

Leaders who pray and stay in tuned to the direction that God wants them will hear from God and offer hope to the hopeless. It is important to pray to God to seek direction for leading his people. All issues are present in our local churches but how many are getting the victory through God's word? The church is the only hospital that many abused women and men will come to and we must begin to address the need for domestic violence services. Domestic violence awareness can and must be incorporated in our Sunday morning messages throughout the year. Propaganda which lists resources for victims of abuse will let members know that this is an issue that the church is concerned about. As we preach that God will deliver from drugs and alcohol, we should preach that he can bring them out of abuse as well.

The Word of God

The word of God instructs a man to love his wife as Christ loved the church. This exemplifies love and care for her and is sealed with his prayers not being hindered. The first scripture that God gave me as I embarked upon this ministry was 1 Samuel 25:1-42. This scripture is an example of a woman who had to save her family in spite of the "foolishness" of her husband. Her husband's response to David's request showed that he had tendencies to be abusive. Abigail interceded for her family's safety because of her husband. This example forced me to look deeper and identify the ways that women have been treated throughout the bible. The word of God is so important. The bible says, "search the scriptures" for in them you think you have eternal life (John 5:39). You can only be sure when you search, because the bible also says that "God rewards those who diligently seek him (Hebrew 11:6)".

After thorough investigation, we will understand 1Peter 3:1 which says, "Likewise, ye wives be in subjection to your own husband that if any obey not the word, they also may without the word be won by the conversation of the wives." We should know that this doesn't mean that women are to allow their husband to treat them any kind of way and that it is acceptable. The scripture is identifying how a woman can win her unsaved husband in how she ministers to him, living the word. The bible also says in 1Peter 3:7-8 "Likewise, ye husbands, dwell with them according to knowledge, giving honor unto the wife, as unto the weaker vessel. Finally, be ye all of one mind having compassion one of another love as the author of confusion, but of power and of love and a sound mind (2Tim. 1:7). When a couple has to end their conversation with one being afraid, it's not God. We must begin teaching men and women how to have a Godly household in spite of their upbringing. It is time that we realize that people don't know how to do things that we assume they do, just because they are grown. In training men and women for marriage the issue of domestic violence generally never comes up.

When a member/leader is found to be in sin he/she is usually "sat down" (which is stricken from all duties he/she holds). However, after counseling for a probation period the member/leader is restored to former duties. But when the offense is Domestic Violence nothing ever happens. They continue in their positions and are not held accountable. Usually, the victim is told to be nicer to her husband, as though she caused the abuse.

We are products of the environment in which we were reared. If a man saw his father beat his mother, he takes this attitude into his manhood and most likely, because of learned behavior, beats his wife. If this behavior is not dealt with, when he becomes a Christian this controlling abusive behavior comes with him. Unless he learns how to control his anger, he will always resort to abuse to get his way. He will justify his wrong doings with the word of God and his upbringing. Many men use the phrase "I am the man of the house and what I say goes" there is no room for God. If a person gets high or drunk, we easily excuse his actions for being led by his substance abuse.

In confronting the issue of domestic violence, we must desire to help by becoming knowledgeable of the word of God concerning the issue. 2Timothy 2:15 says, "Study to show thyself approved unto God a workman that need not to be ashamed, rightly dividing the word of truth." We must begin to minister to the family of God. We are responsible for giving Godly counsel. However, it seems easier to patch up the situation up than to deal with it. There are ways that we can minister that may not always end with separation. But due to severity of the problem the majority of the relationships without continued proper counseling will end.

Although we are talking about how to counsel the abused woman in the church, men are not exempt from being abused. It is detrimental that we teach about the family individual (men, women, and children). We must constantly teach about relationships. For this is what our Lord desires with us, a personal relationship with Christ. If we can't get it right in the natural, what about the spiritual (ICor. 15:46)? We should elaborate on what it means for the woman to be the glory of her husband and what it means to submit.

When we give our lives to the Lord, we must begin to allow the Holy Spirit to guide us in all truth. This would entail re-evaluating some of the things that we were taught about relationship as children.

.

It's time to submit to God and abstain from evil. There is a difference between abuse and submission. God doesn't want to be ever learning and never able to come into the knowledge of the truth (2Tim. 3:7). He has made a way where we can learn from our past mistakes, and put on the whole armor of God (Ephesians 6:11).

The scriptures are filled with incidents of abuse. However, clergy have failed to fully address the issue. One scripture that comes to mind is Psalm 55. This scripture can be used to show that some form of abuse exists in the body of Christ. It says, "it wasn't a stranger who reproached me..." but it was thou a man my equal and my acquaintance, we took sweet counsel together and walked unto the house of God in company". This scripture denotes a relationship with the one who hurt another. Another example of abuse is the scenario described in Judges19 when the concubine and maiden was given over to men to be abused all night. Jesus made his way through the new testament to ensure that women knew that he was for them. He healed the woman who had been bent over for 18 years, the woman at the well, and Mary Magdalene from whom he cast out seven demons. So this is not knew to women, but Jesus made it even clearer when he addressed the crowd surrounding the woman who was caught in adultery, and told them he who is without sin cast the first stone. Many look at these situations as sin only, but to me Jesus let me know that he died for me just like he died for the men who had something to do with these women's conditions. These women were abused physically and sexually.

Counseling

Counseling varies. It can range from a couple visits to long-term ministering. Some women will stay in the abusive relationship and some will leave. They should make the choice. Bringing a couple together to receive counsel is not recommended especially the initial consultation. Factually, this jeopardizes the safety of the victim. Some things that are in joint counseling can do more harm than good.

One of the prerequisites for counseling the abused woman in the church is having the ability to hear from God. The first step to take is to see if the person is safe. Everything else comes after this. When counseling a couple together you will not find out whether the woman is safe because she is going to say what will keep her from being abused when she gets home.

(Special Testimony – The reason that it took me so long to come out of the situation was because, when I got a chance to talk to someone they were just as bad as he was. They wanted to fight him, not understanding that I was right there. Battered women need someone who will read between the lines, and not try to get information in front of the perpetrator. I called the police several times only to be told that they would lock him up for the night and he would be back out. That was no consolation. Also, while in the shelter, the first question wasn't concerning my safety but whether I wanted a divorce. My response was, I want to be safe right now.

Why Does She Stay?

After being delivered from my personal battle with domestic violence, I felt compelled to tackle the question that always has been at the top of this issue. Although it has not been directly answered, society has many instances where a woman has reached out for help and tried to leave to only be murdered, she and her children. The question is still being asked, but no one wants to answer.

In an effort to be sure I give the best answer possible, I started to first take a look at myself and then evaluate the relationship that I was in. Why did I stay? I didn't want to be there but I didn't know how to get out and be safe. So, the first answer that came to me was SAFETY, this is the number one reason women are afraid to leave. Where is Safety? How do I know he won't still harm me, As I remember I realized that I had been deceived into believing that I couldn't get our and if I did then worst would happen. Where could I go that he would not find me? This all boils down to one of the greatest strongholds that satan has placed on women FEAR. Fear grips, torments and holds a person down until they are non-functional. Fear will hinder a person from getting the help they need. However, fear is deceptive in the meaning of the term. These were the questions but the answers had to first come from within me.

I was a victim of domestic violence for two years and there was not a day that went by that I wish I had the strength to leave. It was harder and harder each day, the worse the abuse got the harder it was to leave. I felt that I had no other reason but to stay in the situation. #1 Shame: I married a man twelve years my senior. When the abuse started, I was married for about two weeks and I didn't want anyone to know that this was happening to me and I just got married. Also, allowing a man to hit me symbolized a weakness that I was not ready to show. #2 Pride: I wouldn't dare give family and friends a reason to say they were right or how stupid I was. #3 Fear again: I was afraid of him. The more the battering episodes, the worse they got, the more afraid I became. Fear has a way of paralyzing its victims. This is noticeable in all areas of life. Fear torments. Fear told me that if I left my abuser then he would kill me.

Many women trust that the abuser will change. "Maybe if I changed", Maybe if I didn't talk so much". Some women believe they can change him. "he needs the right woman". There are always survival issues. I was led to believe that the accomplishments I thought that I was making were really nothing according to my abuser. I was going to school, taking care of my daughters, and working every day. I thought that I was finally putting my life in order only to find I was diminished from the verbal abuse I was now suffering. I succumbed under the verbal and emotional abuse. I didn't believe I could make it without him.

Many women start to believe they will never be out. They learn how to tolerate the abusive behavior. It's not that they don't want to get out, they just don't know how. Confiding in local clergy misguided women with misinformation that instructed the abused woman (even myself) to go back into the abuse. There was such a denial of abuse in local congregations that women of God had nowhere to turn.

Approaching the Battered Woman

The battered woman must be approached in love, and not by accusing suggestions that she provoked the altercation. You must not down play any actions. Sometimes we overlook verbal abuse when it can be one of the worst forms of abuse. **Listen** to the woman and **believe her**. Assure her the abuse is not her fault, and is not God's will. This is a time to share scriptures that will define her belief system. Scriptures that will help her embrace God's principles and his love towards her instead of her circumstances. Tell her she is not alone and that help is available. Seek professional help for her. Don't refer her to the marriage outreach or Christian counseling in the local church. She needs individual counseling. She may need a safe place to stay and will probably need to start legal proceedings for her safety. She should not be made to feel as though she is operating out of the will of God if the police are involved.

Hold the abuser accountable for his actions. Don't put his behavior off lightly. Encourage him (if he is available to counseling) to seek help and suggest batterers' counseling for men.

We must minister to her in a way that she feels confident that she is doing what is best for her and her family. She should not be made to feel coerced about any decision that she makes. After going over her options the decisions are solely hers and as counselors we must respect her decision even if it doesn't appear to be the best for the situation.

Some of the relationships will ends in separation and some even divorce. Some may even end up with her going back. It must be her decision. We must allow God to have his perfect work in her life. If separation takes place this could be a time of healing for both parties individually as well as a time to seek help for the children. After such, if restoration is to occur, each person has received the proper counseling that is needed, and each has begun to work on him/herself for the better.

Confidentiality

This is an important asset in counseling abused women. Counselors should be able to keep information confidential. One of the ways that you can assure the client that you will keep her confidence is to sign a confidentiality statement. Christian women pray for God to send someone who they can confide in. Counselors are entrusted with information that is pertinent to the overall healing of the victim. You should not violate anyone's trust. It took a lot for her to come out. You should not discuss cases revealing names, places or anything that would jeopardize her situation. Most of the women who come to men for counseling have had to get up the nerve to overlook that they are talking to a man. So, if this information is misused then it could be detrimental to her deliverance and healing.

If this individual had to leave her home for fear, this information should also be kept confidential. If anyone questions the whereabouts of a person, we should operate under covenant ethics of grace. Just a Rahab did for the men of God which afforded her a place in the hall of faith when she received the spies with peace (Heb. 11:31). If there is immediate danger suspected 911 should be called.

The victim sign a confidentiality statement which suggests the church and those that are under this covenant will not be held responsible by use of unwise tactics of the victim. For example, if he victim stays at a member's home for safety (which is not recommended, but possible), the victim should not contact the abuser and tell her whereabouts. This refuge should remain confidential whether she return to her abuser or not because she may have to use this assistance again.

Staying Focused

No matter how much s situation sounds like yours, you must refrain from interjecting your personal story. Sometimes sharing life experiences can help he client see that someone has gone through similar situations but we don't want to become the client instead of the counselor.

It is very important that we stay focused on what our position as clergy is. We will find that many situations can cause emotions to surface in us. If we are not careful, constantly hearing one side of the story can make us bitter toward the abuser. If the person being counseled comes to the church with her abuser, but she is the only one getting counseled, you will be partial towards her.

Some things that you will hear can also make you want to take matters into your hands. This is forbidden. Our main goal should be to help this woman get on the road to healing.

When possible we must try to bring both parties together. A house divided against itself cannot stand (Mark 3:25). The goal is to do whatever we can do to help this family stay together. Sometimes this is impossible especially when the spouse is unsaved.

Know when to refer. Everyone cannot counsel everybody. It is important to know that no matter how much you may want to help a person, if you are in unfamiliar territory, or you find the client clinging to you in an unhealthy manner (looking to you as a savior instead of God) the best resource is to refer. You must analyze the situation, pray and ask the Holy Spirit to guide you.

Goal of Victim Assistant in the Local Church

Empower each women with the ability to make changes in her life that would lead to her experiencing freedom in Christ Jesus that he desires for her.

Resources

Whenever this publication is used you should have local literature, support groups, and general information about abuse. This will help you stay informed and will serve as a guide to helping church members.

Theological and scriptural homework will allow you to better understand and respond to family violence. Also, receiving training from professional in the field of domestic violence counseling can be a great asset to your congregation. Make your church a safe place where victims of domestic can come for help. Display brochures and posters which include telephone numbers of domestic violence programs in your area.

Educate the congregation. Provide ways for members of the congregation to learn as much as they can about domestic violence. Start a support group in your local church. Invite staff from local domestic violence programs to make educational presentation.

Brady Solutions is in the process of establishing Domestic Violence Outreach Center in local churches. If you would like to have a Domestic Violence Outreach Center in your church and would like for Brady Solutions to assist you please give us a call at 202-644-6741. This will include training for support group sessions. This will give you the ability to minister to women who are in abusive relationships and are seeking a Godly answer.

.

Today, I pastor Survival Temple Church. I assist Church leaders with setting up domestic violence outreach ministries in the local church. I train clergy who will assist and counsel battered women. I also conduct a seminar entitled, "Breaking the Cycle of Domestic Violence within the Body of Christ". Since the Lord has brought me out of bondage, I have a yearning to address not only those who don't know Him as their personal savior. I want all to know that abuse in not acceptable to God under any conditions. This behavior cannot go on in the Church. There are many people, including clergy, who are aware of abuse and don't know how to deal with it. God has given me patience, which is a beneficial asset in counseling, and firsthand knowledge of what it means to be abused. I am here to let you know that help is available. Help is all around us. We must become educated to what God has given us and use it.

This book was written to enlighten and strengthen the women of God, both those who are standing in the shadows and those who have been delivered. God has not given us the spirit of fear but of power, and of love, and of a sound mind (2 Tim. 1:7). "I Survived" is dedicated to the women who are persevering to be obedient to the Lord, and revere His divine order.

Deliverance, grace and mercy allows me to tell my story in order to help others who might be in a similar situation to mine, or, now that they have been delivered, are wondering what they can do to help others.

I am now a contact person to various domestic violence shelters in the area for those who have concerns about counseling a woman of God. I have also been able to help ministers and pastors to encourage the abused women in their local churches

I finally have it: the closeness, the joy, the peace, and, yes, the security that I longed for in the Lord. The time has finally come when I feel complete and settled in Jesus. I knew even on the worst days that God loved me and that He would never let anything happen to me that I couldn't bear. I knew that He was with me every step of the way. I know that I could not have made it through everything that I suffered, everything that I endured, without God. No one could have convinced me that I would be able to survive the pain, suffering, verbal, physical, mental, and spiritual abuse that I have gone through. To God be the glory: I made it. **I SURVIVED! YOU CAN TOO.**

EPILOGUE

Survival Strategies

As you can see the road to success after abuse is not as easy as it may appear. However, it can be done. With God, all things are possible. (Matthew 19:26)

When making plans to leave domestic violence, major strategies have to be considered. Strategizing will reduce the chances of returning. A plan of escape and if possible a buddy system with someone you can trust are essential. It is very important to maintain personal papers such as birth certificates, social security cards and health records. Also, any background information on the perpetrator would be extremely helpful when seeking legal assistance. It is not recommended to seek shelter with relatives or friends that the perpetrator knows. Victims who are serious about leaving and never returning should consider moving as far away as possible. This lessens the ability for her abuser to find them and allows them to experience a true sense of freedom when considering options of returning.

Making the decision to leave can be hard based on the mixed emotions the victim is experiencing. No doubt, the perpetrator is telling her how much he loves her, he needs her, and how he won't do it again. Fear is yet present. The decision to divorce is being considered especially if there are any children involved. She could also still love him and not want her family divided. These feelings and emotions are valid. The woman in the church thinks of her husband's status. She doesn't want to make him look bad. She is taught that what goes on at home should stay in the home. The bible says, whatever is done in darkness will come to the light (1 Cor. 4:5). Who better to bring it out than the victim. This will not only help her, but it may cause him to get the help he needs to keep the family together.

Although many victims are women there are men who are being abused. The abuse weighs the same. No one should live in a home with a person and not be free. Men must help other men. If women help women and they become freed, what about the men? The house is yet divided until he gets the help he needs.

Abuse is running rampant in our local churches, and we need to acknowledge and deal with it. The bible says, "we are to submit to one another", we are joint heirs together with Christ. When you (man) take on a wife, the two become one flesh, you must treat your wife as Christ loves the church, and He gave his life for us (Ephesians 5:21,25,31&33).

In order for the woman of God to gain enough strength and courage to come out of domestic violence she must first seek the face of God. One thing that is pertinent to her survival is prayer. She must realize that God is not the perpetrator. God did not give her this individual. God is not the author of confusion.

Secondly, she must confess her faults no matter how small. If she knows that marrying this person was out of the will of God, she needs to repent. This prepares her for total sanctification before God. Lastly, she must surrender to God. This will say to God, not my will, but your will be done in my life.

She must not focus on her perpetrator; she must practice the presence of God. In essence she must dwell on how God would want her to live. Would God want her to suffer this way? She needs to study the word of God and begin to see herself as God sees her. Find scriptures of strength to hold on to. Know that God says, you are "fearfully and wonderfully made" (Psalm 139:14); you are a royal priesthood, a peculiar people (1 Peter 2:9). The Bible also declares that God will never leave you nor forsake you (Heb. 13:5).

This will help her to learn who she is in the sight of God. The perpetrator has put her down and damaged her self-esteem. Now, she must allow the Word of God show her that she is special, that she is fearfully and wonderfully made (Psalm 139:14).

Following this method will surely encourage her spiritually, and will allow her to see herself in a different light. No matter how many bruises she has, she should wash her face and see what God sees, beauty. Beauty is not only outward. The woman was not an afterthought. God made her compatible to man with emphasis that he gives to her, which assisted in taking his mind off of himself. She also has power, only to be tapped into.

Are You Being Abused?

Every twelve seconds in this country a woman is beaten or injured by the man she lives with and loves. More women seek emergency treatment for injuries caused by their husbands or partners than from rape, car accidents and muggings combined. This abuse is particularly heinous when it exists with the Body of Christ. I can tell you from my own experience that sincere and committed women of God are being abused in the name of the Lord. Misinterpretation of scriptures such as, "Likewise ye wives be in subjection…" (1 Peter 3:1) has heightened the defense of the perpetrator. Scriptural misinterpretation and gender orientation can mislead and cause harm if we fail to rightly divide the word of God.

While it is true that God has a divine order, we are to revere one another. We must use wisdom and knowledge if we are to be in accordance with the Word of God. The Bible says, in Ephesians 5:25, (Husband, love your wives, even as Christ also loved the church and gave himself for it).

Abusers cause fear and confusion. God is not the author of confusion, but he has given us peace (1 Corin. 14:33). "For God hath not given us the spirit of fear; but of power and of love, and of a sound mind…" (2 Tim. 1:7). Abuse is contrary to the word of God. We are to acknowledge the Lord in all our ways and he will direct our paths.

If you are being abused, don't keep it a secret. Talk about it! The following questions are some ways to help you determine if you are a victim of abuse.

Does he:
1. Keep track of all of your time?
2. Keep you isolated from outside contact?
3. Accuse you of being unfaithful?
4. Discourage your relationships with family and friends?
5. Prevent you from working or going back to school?
6. Criticize you or humiliate you in front of others?
7. Anger easily without being provoked?
8. Belittle things that are important to you?
9. Hit, slap or punch you or your children?
10. Threaten to use a weapon against you?
11. Do bodily harm?
12. Force you to have sex against your will?

If you find yourself saying yes to any of these questions, you should seek help today. For shelter referrals, please call the Battered Women's Shelter in your area. This number can be found by dialing 411. If you are in immediate danger, please call 911.

Scriptural References from KJV

Genesis 3:16 ● St. Matthews 21:1-15 ● St. John 4:29
St. Matthews 21:2-3 ● I Peter 3:1 ● I Peter 2:9 ● I
Timothy 2:11-12
St. Mark 8:34 ● Galatians 3:26-29 ● Genesis 2:24 ●
Isaiah 54:17
Genesis 1:27 ● Philippians 2:12 ● I John 5:3 ● Romans
7:2
Ephesians 5:28-29 ● Ephesians 5:21, 25, 31 & 33 ● St.
John 11:28
I Thessalonians 5:17 ● Proverbs 15:1 ● St. Matthews
12:25
Psalm 139:14 ● Hebrews 13:5 ● 2 Timothy 1:7 ● I
Corinthians 4:5

The Bottom Line

This is a guide. It is designed to give you an idea of how to assist those in the local church or visit and need assistance. This information gives a general overview of how this issue can be handled without violated confidentiality and deter the situation from becoming dangerous.

Be prepared to serve. The lack of service and communication in the local assembly is what is keeping women in bondage. Speak out more than once a year.

Resources – We must have Resources; local shelter numbers and contacts; hotel stipend for those emergencies that need to shelter women and children for a few nights.

Put Pamplets in the Bathroom at the church with important number or design a place where a person can leave a request for help.

Safety Instructions – Have Monthly Meetings evaluating a safety Plan.

Be Empathetic – She doesn't need to know your story – Hear Hers.

This Happened it doesn't Matter How – Don't Add to her; listen.

There Are Not Enough 2nd Phase Shelters For Women To Start Over – Lets Be Innovative in Serving Our Communities

Do Not Treat Domestic Violence as Marriage Counseling

Believe Her – Believe Her – Believe Her

Apostle Adrianne D. Brady

Apostle Brady established Survival Temple Word of Faith Church and Brady Solutions LLC located in Capital Heights, MD. She is a widow and the mother of five adult children and grandmother of seven. She is the Pastor of Kingdom Refuge Ministries International in District Heights, MD.

Pastor Brady was married to a preacher who abused her for two years. While in the abusive relationship and seeking help from various churches she realized the help for the woman in the church was and still is very limited. She found herself seeking a Godly answer and wasn't very successful. Different pastors told her that she should go home and work on her marriage. After the Lord delivered her, she was led of God to go back to help the women who are being left out (the women in the church).

Through this experience she started conducting seminars, workshops, and an annual conference entitled "Breaking the Cycle of Domestic Violence Within the Body of Christ". This also initiated the writing of her first book "I Survived" True Encounter of a Battered Woman and the start of I Survived Outreach Ministry.

Pastor Brady has traveled extensively over the years speaking on the issue of domestic violence in the church. She has participated in various women's meetings and programs. Her speaking engagements have taken her throughout the Baltimore-Washington area as well as

Virginia, Pennsylvania, Delaware, Massachusetts, Missouri, Ohio, and North Carolina. She has participated in panel discussions representing clergy and domestic violence as well as board meetings of local shelters. She was also contacted by the Oprah Winfrey Show and appeared in a Documentary called "Any Day Now" in Charlotte, NC.

Through the leading of the Holy Ghost, Pastor Brady has comprised a training package specifically for the Body of Christ which also includes her latest book, How to Counsel the Abused Woman in the Church. Churches who are interested in starting a domestic violence outreach center in their local church would find Pastor Brady's training and expertise in this area very helpful. In order to combat this growing device God has instructed her to start a ministry to cater to women with low self-esteem, despair and those who need a push to get them moving. This ministry business name is Brady Solution whose moto is "Inspired to Serve". This organization is designed to train, instruct, and mentor those who have a desire grow in God and seek their purpose. If you would like to speak to Apostle Adrianne Brady, please feel free to contact her at (240)280-9884 or email: bradysolution@gmail.com

www.ingramcontent.com/pod-product-compliance
Lightning Source LLC
Chambersburg PA
CBHW051713090426
42736CB00013B/2683